Sadie - The Caring Lady

Justyne Anderson

Sadie - The Caring Lady
Copyright © 2023 by Justyne Anderson

All rights reserved. No part of this publication may be reproduced, distributed, or transmitted in any form or by any means, including photocopying, recording, or other electronic or mechanical methods, without the prior written permission of the author, except in the case of brief quotations embodied in critical reviews and certain other non-commercial uses permitted by copyright law.

Tellwell Talent
www.tellwell.ca

ISBN
978-0-2288-5408-1 (Hardcover)
978-0-2288-5407-4 (Paperback)

This book is dedicated to my beautiful son, Lachlan James McMillan Hume.

Sadie was a nurse and worked in a hospital. Sadie just loved caring for others.

Sadie cared for others when she worked and she cared for others when she wasn't at work, such as her family.

All in all Sadie loved caring for other people.

Sadie would start her day at work looking after sick people.

She would help them wash, help them dress and give them their medicine to help them get better.

She would sometimes sit with them and listen to how they were feeling.

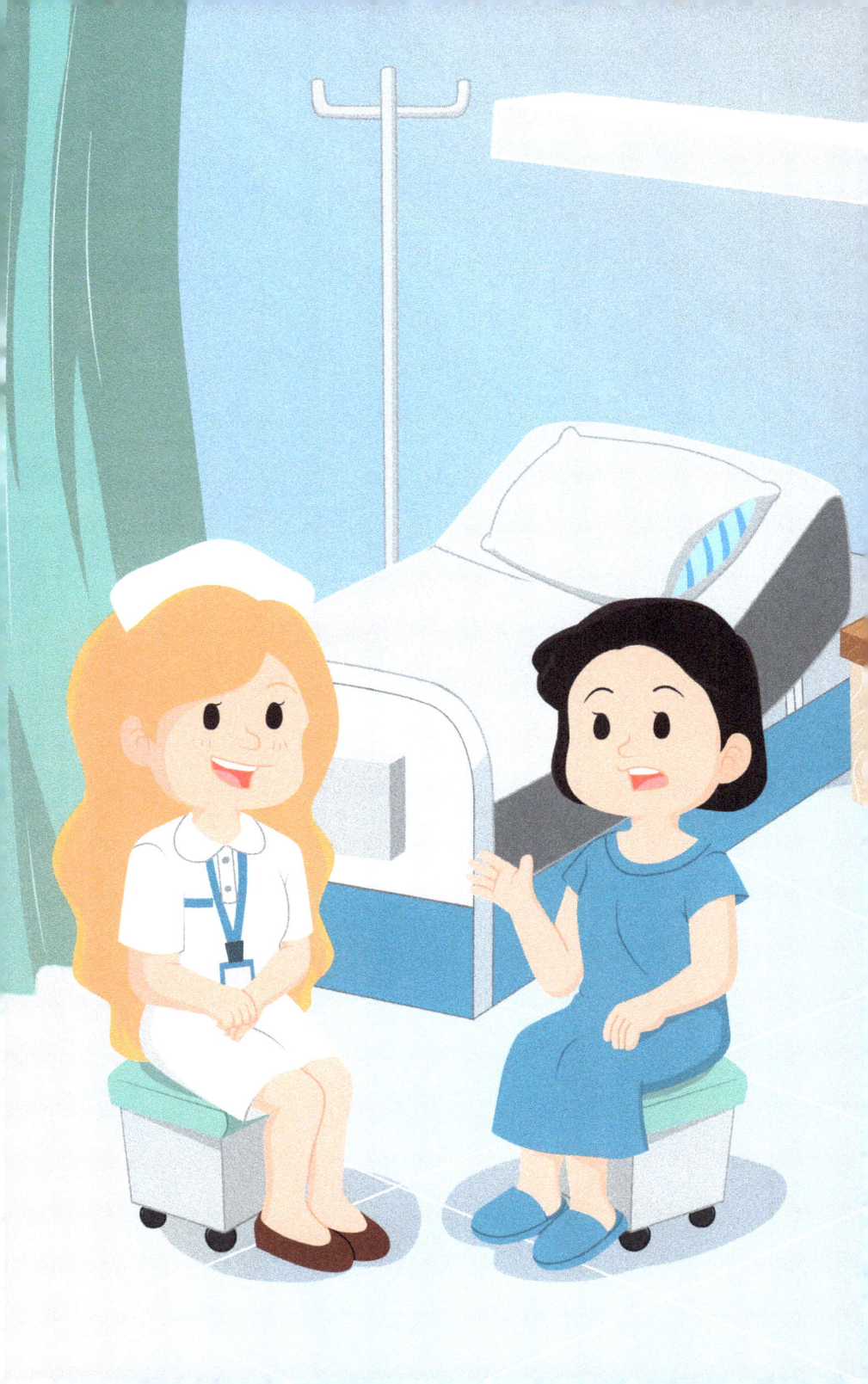

Some of the patients didn't have any friends or family to do that with so Sadie would enjoy hearing their stories.

Sometimes they would cry to Sadie because they were so sick so Sadie would make sure they know that everything would be ok.

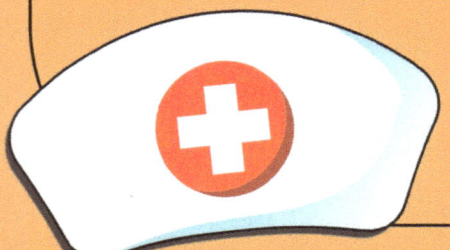

She listened to them because she was such a caring nurse.

Sadie would end her day very, very tired for all the caring she did.

Sadie needed to sleep now so she could do it all over again because that's what Sadie enjoyed doing each and every day.

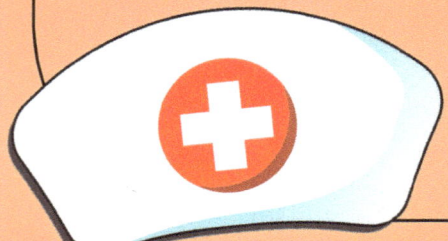

Sadie woke up thinking about all the people she wanted to care for that day.

Where would she start?

Maybe at the hospital with her patients?

Or maybe at home with her family?

Sadie loved to care for her family too.

Each and every day she would tell her children how much she loved them and that she would do anything to care for them.

All in all, Sadie cared for somebody each and every day.

So that's why everyone called her Sadie the Caring Lady!

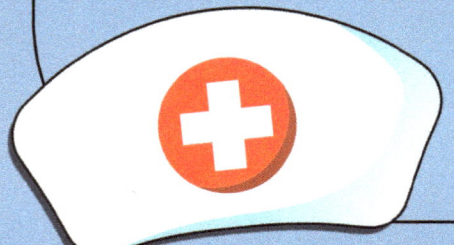

I want to dedicate this book to all the wonderful, kind, and compassionate people that I have had caring for me during my illness over the past few years. I cannot feel more grateful for the kindness and support I have received.

www.ingramcontent.com/pod-product-compliance
Lightning Source LLC
LaVergne TN
LVHW051936070526
838200LV00077B/4645